.... WHAT'S AT ISSUE? ....

MAKING A DIFFERENCE

Richard Spilsbury

Heinemann
LIBRARY

www.heinemann.co.uk/library
Visit our website to find out more information about **Heinemann Library** books.

To order:
 Phone 44 (0) 1865 888066
 Send a fax to 44 (0) 1865 314091
Visit the Heinemann Bookshop at www.heinemann.co.uk/library to browse our catalogue and order online.

First published in Great Britain by Heinemann Library, Halley Court, Jordan Hill, Oxford OX2 8EJ, a division of Reed Educational and Professional Publishing Ltd. Heinemann is a registered trademark of Reed Educational & Professional Publishing Limited.

OXFORD MELBOURNE AUCKLAND JOHANNESBURG BLANTYRE
GABORONE IBADAN PORTSMOUTH NH (USA) CHICAGO

Designed by Tinstar Design (www.tinstar.co.uk)
Originated by Ambassador Litho Ltd
Printed in Hong Kong/China

ISBN 0 431 03555 5

05 04 03 02 01
10 9 8 7 6 5 4 3 2 1

British Library Cataloguing in Publication Data
Spilsbury, Richard
      Making a difference. – (What's at issue?)
      1. Charities – Juvenile literature
      I. Title
      361.7

Acknowledgements
The Publishers would like to thank the following for permission to reproduce photographs:
Associated Press: p15; Comic Relief: p42; Corbis: Penny Tweedie p4, Neil Rabinowitz p5, David Turnley p7, Adrian Arbib p12, Mark Kettenhofer p17, Howard Davies p19, Annie Griffiths Belt p20, Galen Rowell p32, Kevin Schafer p39; Cumulus: pp10, 22, Daniel Bosler: p27; David Woodfall p30; Rex Features: pp24, 36, Nils Jorgensen pp9, 35, Tony Kyriacou p13, Fernado Cavalcanti p16, Paul Brown p25; Richard Spilsbury: p41; Tony Stone Images: Paul Edmondson p34; Trip: H Rogers p29; WWF: p11

Cover photograph: Rex Features.

Any words appearing in the text in bold, **like this**, are explained in the Glossary.

Contents

Introduction

Making a difference to the lives of others and the world around us can happen at many different levels. It can be putting a coin in a collecting box, doing some shopping or gardening for an elderly person, or **campaigning** outside government buildings. It can be a short- or a long-term act. It can be local or international. There are also many issues involved. Should charity begin at home or should it be given wherever there is a need in the world? Does helping people stop them helping themselves? Can individuals really make a difference in the face of massive global problems? Do voluntary actions and organizations allow governments to avoid their responsibilities to their **citizens**? This book is a starting point for exploring your own attitudes towards contributing money, time, skills and energy and how we can all make a difference.

Why should we make a difference?

There are around six billion people on Earth. Clean water, a safe environment, protection from violence and **equal opportunities** are basic **human rights**. But millions of people are denied one or more of these rights. We can also add to this list the right to have enough food to eat; access to healthcare; primary schooling for all children; work and free speech. Yet more than 800 million people do not have enough food to stay healthy and 900 million people cannot read or write.

All of us crave safety in our health, relationships, security and future.

A divided world?

The world is divided into developed and developing countries. Developed countries are those where large-scale industry, based on burning **fossil fuels** like oil and coal, are well established and usually the main source of jobs and wealth creation. Developing countries, on the other hand, are those where farming is still the main way of life. People in developed countries are usually richer on average than people in developing countries. When looked at in more detail though, some people in developed countries are very rich and many others are very poor, without homes, jobs or enough food to eat. Different countries, whatever their wealth, have different priorities about what to spend their money on. For example, Cuba, a very poor country, has equivalent or better primary healthcare than the much richer North America.

Many industries are changing rapidly, with increasing technology and **global trading**. Once stable industries, like farming and coal mining, are now at risk from cheaper **imports** which means many farmers and miners are now unemployed and slipping further into poverty. These effects can hit developing countries more than developed countries: people's needs and rights suffer. Millions of children die from the effects of diarrhoea each year because of poor sanitation. Drinking a mixture of clean water, sugar and salts can prevent it easily and very cheaply, yet some countries are too poor to provide this themselves.

FACTS

- *620 million have died since 1945 from lack of food, safe water and basic healthcare*
- *60,000 people, on average, in East Africa share just one doctor*
- *24 years is, on average, how much longer North Americans live than Africans*
- *7% of babies in the developing world die before their first birthday*
- *20% of the world's people earn 75% of the world's income.*

Sadly, many of us spend a lot of our time ignoring the needs of our fellow human beings and our shared environment. We often think of ourselves, take advantage of each other's difficulties and sometimes act with cruelty and violence towards each other. People do, however, have a range of tools that can help solve problems. We have developed laws and **cultures** which set rules for human behaviour. We use science and technology to make life easier, less routine and safer. We have access to large amounts of information and many tools for communicating. Yet many people, many other species of plants and animals, many **ecosystems** and environments are struggling to survive.

In a highly-populated world with massive problems like hunger, poverty, cruelty and environmental destruction,

it is sometimes difficult to see how we, as individuals, can make a difference. But it is possible to help make your village, your country, or even your world, a better place. We can act as responsible **citizens** by putting just some of our time and energy into helping others less fortunate than ourselves. This book looks at some of the ways in which we can make a difference.

The contrast between living conditions for rich and poor people can be extreme.

Is the world a less caring place?

We often view much older societies as more primitive than present ones. We think we have advanced in so many ways. However, one sign of a civilized society or **culture** is its efforts to look after its less fortunate members. Traditional Australian Aboriginal culture, for example, believes strongly in **kinship** ties, a society based on duty to family and to a selfless, sharing system of living. Another example is ancient Greece and Rome, where there were laws to help the old and ill in newly formed cities.

Many modern governments also set aside resources to give to the poor and needy, at home and abroad. Society is changing, though. There are ever-greater numbers of people on the planet putting more and more pressure on governments' money. More people are unemployed or underemployed, many are caught in poverty and there are growing problems like drug abuse and environmental issues.

Who cares?

Governments can do so much, but with limited finances they rely on the efforts of individuals and groups who volunteer time and effort to help fill in the gaps that the government cannot cover. In fact, **non-governmental organizations (NGOs)** often provide much-valued direction to governments. Their independence helps them take a more objective view of problems in society, and by focusing on particular problems they are able to get things done efficiently. The **campaigning** of a few caring people can therefore make a big difference to the rights and lives of many. Some people believe that governments do not do enough and that in an ideal world there would be no need for NGOs. They claim that volunteers helping others lets governments 'off the hook' from their responsibilities.

Should charity begin at home?

Some people cannot understand the desire to volunteer money, time or energy to help others. They say that we pay **taxes** to our governments in part to aid the needy, so there is no need to get involved and that, anyway, there are lots of people who do not even try to help themselves. They might back up this argument with stories of people who try to get more money out of the welfare system than they have a right to, for example people who work while also claiming benefits. Others might be happy to help charities in their own country but disagree with helping people in other countries. They might argue that big overseas problems like famine are simply proof of '**survival of the fittest**', and that it is not our duty to help people somewhere else when we have enough problems in our own society. They feel that help should come from the governments of the countries affected. What do you think?

However, others feel that it is vital for the planet as a whole that we see ourselves, not just as **citizens** of the community or

country where we live, but also as **global** citizens. This is because everything in the world is linked. By polluting the sea in one country you could be affecting beaches on the other side of the world; by campaigning for civil rights for one group of people in one country you could

> It is surprisingly easy to walk past and ignore those less fortunate than ourselves.

be making it easier for people in another country to set up their own. Where do you stand on these issues?

A BRIEF HISTORY OF CHARITY AND PHILANTHROPY

People often talk about Christian charity, but many other faiths and cultures have also wanted to help others. 4000 years ago the Babylonian King Hammurabi ordered that 'justice be done to widows, orphans and the poor'. Moses set up the tithe system so that a tenth of any harvest would be given to the poor. Buddhism is a religion based on self-control and charity to the poor. Many religious faiths tell stories of early saints and missionaries who helped others while spreading the word about their faith. Later religious groups established **almshouses**, orphanages and missions all over the world to look after less fortunate people. Rich industrialists at the turn of the 20th century, seeing the struggle of many in a more and more populated and industrialized world, set up charitable foundations for the benefit of humanity.

Religion is still a major motive behind charity across the world. Of the $144 billion given to non-profit organizations in the USA in 1998, $116 billion was given to religions and churches.

Some people argue, however, that all this benevolence has a hidden agenda: to encourage people to change their belief system, or to move them from the fringes of society into the mainstream where they can be more easily controlled. What do you think?

How do people make a difference?

Many people volunteer their time, energy or money to help others. One person might visit an old, frail neighbour a couple of times a week, getting shopping, chatting or organizing transport to a doctor's appointment. Another person might spend a few hours collecting money on the street for a national charity that provides care for the elderly in general. Both people are making a difference to the lives of old people, but one prefers to help a particular person, while the other is happy to help in a more general way.

Charities

Many charities are organizations formed to help people, animals and **habitats** in need. They raise funds for their particular activities by collecting money and other **donations** from individuals and from businesses. Charities exist at local, national and international levels. They may concentrate on a wide range of **campaigns** or they may have a much more limited scope.

Charities help people in many different ways, for example by:
- relieving financial hardship (giving money, food, clothing, housing and other help)
- promoting education (providing playgroups, work-related training and research institutions)
- supporting religion (looking after places of worship, paying church ministers or holding services)
- benefiting the community in other ways (non-financial help for old, sick or disabled people, promoting racial harmony, providing leisure facilities, and so on).

Many charities employ paid staff. Some workers provide direct services, such as the professional inspectors who check on animals in trouble for the RSPCA, or the nurses who work for Macmillan Cancer Relief. Other charity workers help to get more money for their cause. They do this by writing and designing effective appeals for donations. They talk to governments, businesses and the media about the cause, campaigning for changes in law and in public awareness. They also coordinate the efforts of volunteers and work with other charities.

There are also millions of charity volunteers across the world who give up their time and energy to help others. People volunteer for charities in many different ways: from advice worker, campaigner or fundraiser to handyperson, driver or cook. Some give a few minutes a week while others may spend most of their lives volunteering.

Non-governmental organizations

All charities are **non-governmental organizations (NGOs)** because their purposes and fundraising are independent of government help. Non-charitable NGOs can be local groups,

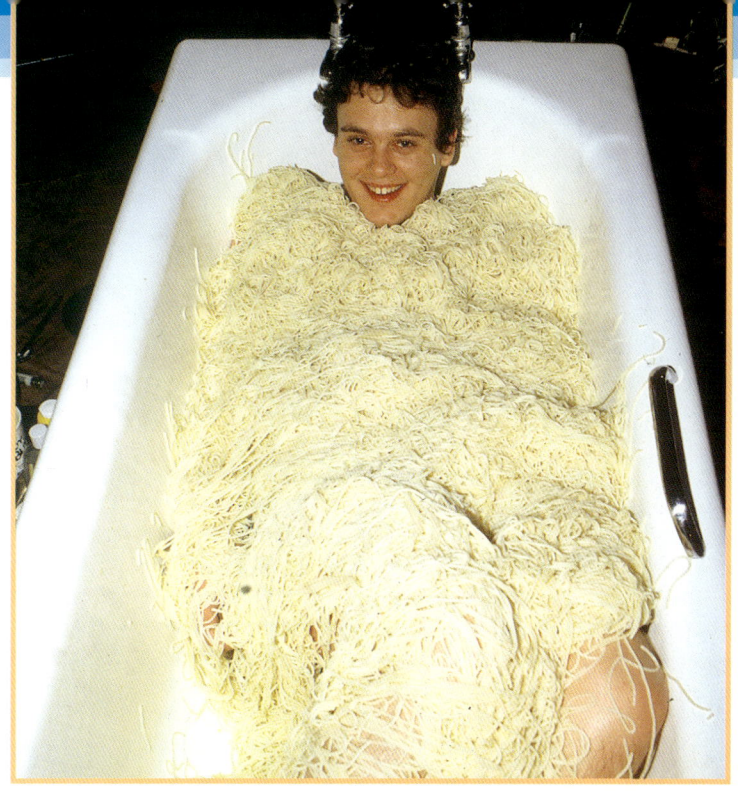

Wacky ideas, like bathing in spaghetti, can be put to good use in fundraising.

such as Green Business Networks, which promote the exchange of ideas and skills between businesses in order to make their activities more environmentally friendly. They can also be massive bodies such as the International Monetary Fund (IMF), a **cooperative** of 182 countries which aims to maintain a stable world currency system, so that **currency** payments between countries take place smoothly, and which also gives out loans to aid poor countries.

Fundraising

When you go shopping you decide that you want to spend your money on a particular product. In the same way, when you give money to a charity you are deciding to contribute to a particular cause. This might be quite a general cause, such as advancing cancer research, or it might be more specific, such as giving money for rebuilding a church roof. After a natural disaster, many different charities have appeals to raise money specifically for the victims and the people who give their money want to know that it is going to those victims. In many countries charities are registered so that governments can make sure that they use their money in the ways they say they will. All charities should work for the benefit of the public and not particular individuals and the money they collect should be spent on what it was given for.

FUNDRAISING ON THE INTERNET

Apart from the well-known sponsored fasts, bungee jumps, bed pushes, marathons and head shaves, there are new ways to raise funds for charities. Originality is the key in an overcrowded charity market. At www.handbag.com there is an on-line auction of famous people's handbags for charity. Baroness Thatcher's handbag raised £100,000 in aid of Breast Cancer Care. Sinead O'Connor made the first Internet-only charity single for the Warchild charity.

FACTS

● *At the end of 1998 there were 188,476 charities on the UK Charities Commission Register with a total annual income of £19,749,690,739.*
● *People tend to give to familiar charities: 5% of charities receive over 85% of the total annual income recorded.*
● *70% of registered charities have an income of £10,000 or less each year.*

Helping others or helping ourselves?

When we help others are we really giving generously, or is it simply a way of helping ourselves? Some people argue that when you put money into a homeless person's collection you are helping that person by being **altruistic**. This means you do it with no regard for yourself, only for the good of the other person. Others explain everything people do in terms of the idea of the 'selfish gene'. This means that whatever we do, we are always looking out for 'number one'. They say that giving money can make you feel good because you have helped someone else, but also that it makes you feel less guilty about not putting money into the next person's collecting box. Some people also think that by helping someone else we are perhaps more likely to be helped ourselves if in need in the future.

On Red Nose Day, television spectacle is interrupted by calls for donations in a carefully balanced mix of fun and seriousness.

Giving and receiving

It is true that some people expect something in return for their act of giving, perhaps a sticker or balloon, or an entertaining event. In the UK, Comic Relief organizes a Red Nose Day every two years. Media stars give their time to encourage people to give money to charity, with a special emphasis on having fun while giving. But why should giving be a fun thing? Aren't we forgetting the misery in some people's lives? Is fooling about really appropriate when serious issues such as disability and children's poverty are involved? Are we just raising the profiles of stars who will do anything to stay in the public eye?

National lottery schemes in many countries encourage people to give in return for a numbered ticket that might make them rich if it is picked. A portion of the money raised in such schemes goes to charities. Some people say you could help charities more by giving directly to them, or by having smaller prizes for winners. But others argue that without the promise of riches, people wouldn't bother putting money into the scheme. What do you think?

Causes and effects

Many people prefer to do voluntary work because they get to spend time with other volunteers, while at the same time contributing to a selected cause. Volunteering can then be both a cause and a social club. Others start voluntary groups because they are interested in a particular cause and, by encouraging others to chip in, they are, in a way, furthering their own ends. For example, up until the late 19th century, women were not allowed to vote. A few **suffragettes** in different countries volunteered their time and energy to perform dramatic acts that would bring attention to the unfairness of this and eventually the laws were changed.

We all have different amounts of energy, money and time that we are able to or want to spend on helping others. Constant demands for giving might irritate us and make us less likely to give. Endless reports on TV and radio, collectors on the street and envelopes through the letterbox can quickly lead to '**compassion fatigue**'. We may not have much money or time to give and could be made to feel guilty for not helping. While it is 'the thought that counts', we all have to ask ourselves how much we are prepared to do to help others in more practical ways.

A RECOGNIZED BRAND

As many charities do similar or overlapping work – sometimes helping the same groups of people – it can be vital for a charity to be instantly recognizable. People are more likely to put their money in the collecting box of a charity they know than one they have never heard of. Branding is the art of making individual and attractive qualities prominent. A breakfast cereal manufacturer might make its product appear healthier to eat by putting pictures of people exercising or fresh fruit on the packet. A charity also creates a particular look by: using a distinctive **logo**; writing press advertisements or requests for money using particular language; designing posters in a particular style; or associating with recognizable media personalities. What charities can you think of that have an instantly recognizable brand?

WWF

Protests and pressure groups

How far would you go to fight for something you believe in? If you think that whaling is wrong would you sign a petition, or would you join a **demonstration** outside government buildings? Or perhaps you can sympathise with people who board boats and put themselves in between the whales and the whalers' harpoon guns? Some people would go to any lengths to help the cause they believe in.

Road protestors and construction workers clash.

Emotive issues

It is often the case that strong, active protests centre on **emotive** or controversial issues. Many people defend fox hunting because it has been going on for centuries and is part of life in the countryside. They are angry that people who they feel don't understand their way of life try to impose their values on them. But many others believe fox hunting is an out-dated sport that causes unnecessary pain to the foxes. Hunt protestors try to peacefully disrupt hunts but with feelings running high, fights can sometimes break out between hunters and protestors, with police in the middle.

Other groups are violently opposed to human **abortion**. They say that to kill a tiny embryo is no different from killing a baby. In some countries, doctors who believe in a mother's right to decide to abort her child, for whatever reason, get death threats from anti-abortionists.

TRAFFIC TROUBLES

Many people use a car to travel around, and some rely on a car to earn a living. Many drivers are demanding new roads to cut down on the traffic jams that fill major motorways and city streets at rush hour. Road protestors try to stop road developments because they care about the habitats that are destroyed when the new roads are built. Some protestors live in tree-house communities for weeks preventing the work of the loggers and bulldozers. Protestors who take direct action of this sort are often young. Some people think that certain causes attract young people because they give them a chance to live at the **dissenting** edge of society and even to be seen as stylish. But other people believe that strong protest can and should come from all ages because many problems that need to be addressed affect us all.

Violent protests

There are those who believe that some people join violent or illegal protest groups because it gives them the chance to do violent or illegal things with the excuse of doing them for a cause. But what if the laws that have been set need to be questioned? For example, some people disagree strongly with carrying out scientific and medical research on animals. They feel that the rights of animals are as important as those of people. Some groups of **animal liberationists** are prepared to break into **laboratories** and release imprisoned animals. Others have even sent letter bombs to employees of **pharmaceutical** companies that use animals in experiments. But can breaking the law in this way ever be right?

Putting on the pressure

There are many ways of protesting about things you don't agree with. Genetically modified (GM) foods are made from **organisms** whose **genetic** content has been artificially changed by scientists. Many people believe that GM food was not tested enough before it started to be sold in shops. They fear it could have unknown effects on health and on other organisms and **ecosystems**. Following peaceful **campaigns** from a variety of **pressure groups**, many supermarkets have decided not to sell food containing GM ingredients. However, the profile of the cause was undoubtedly raised by pressure groups that destroyed test fields of GM crops.

Raising awareness of issues like destruction of the environment, be it trees threatened by road construction, or arctic wildlife threatened by oil exploration, can take many forms.

These acts were publicized in the media and although many questioned the right to destroy other people's crops, they focused public attention on the issue. Organizations such as Greenpeace call for a ban on GM food but also seek to promote organic food and more widespread changes in eating practices through their *True Food Campaign*.

Voluntary groups contribute much to putting pressure on other people and governments to make changes. People set up stalls on busy shopping streets and encourage people to sign petitions and pick up information about their cause. Others join in marches and large-scale rallies, combining passionate protest with the chance to share a fun day out with like-minded people.

Freedom of speech

Most people believe that we have the right to voice our own opinions. But for some people in the world, saying what you think can be a very dangerous thing. In some countries, governments do not believe that their people should have the chance to vote in free and fair elections, or to peacefully protest against laws they don't agree with. In fact, those people who do, or might, protest are considered dangerous and are often imprisoned without fair trial and tortured or even killed. In China in 1989, a peaceful student protest calling for **democracy** ended in the government sending in tanks and soldiers to stop the protest, killing many protestors.

During times of armed conflict, those who think that violence is not the way to solve the problems between countries are called 'conscientious objectors'. Many conscientious objectors have been imprisoned because they are considered traitors to a country's war effort.

Media power

Newspapers, TV, radio and the Internet together form the media. Opinions about a whole range of issues are expressed in the media and influence other people's ideas. The media can be a powerful aid to any cause. In some countries the media is completely controlled by the government and so promotes only the government's views. In others, it is controlled by only one section of society, sometimes the majority, but at other times just the section with the most power. In Rwanda in 1994 state-controlled radio broadcasts helped to start violence between two **ethnic** groups in the country – the Hutu, who were in power, and the Tutsi. In just three violent months, around one million Rwandans were killed, the majority by state-trained Hutu **militia**, and three million fled the violence as **refugees** to neighbouring countries.

Censorship

In other countries there is a wide range of uncontrolled media. Some people say that free speech is not always a good thing. What if you were surfing the Internet and came across disturbing images of violence against children, messages promoting racial hatred or instructions on how to make bombs? Is it a good thing that dangerous ideas like these can be freely available in this way? Shouldn't we have ways of controlling what it is acceptable to say or who sees what images?

UNITED NATIONS

The United Nations (UN) is an international organization with members from a large number of countries around the world. Its purpose is to maintain peace and security across the world. It tries to get countries to talk to each other about their differences rather than use force. The 1948 UN Universal Declaration of Human Rights defined certain rights and freedoms that everyone in the world should be entitled to. One of these rights is the freedom to hold opinions and be able to speak about them without fear. More than 50 years later many people are still struggling to achieve this basic human right.

There are some restrictions on what people see, from systems for teachers or parents to control what children see on the Internet, to film censors putting age restrictions on films. But some people say that any **censorship** is dangerous because everyone has the right to make up their own mind and not be restricted by others. What do you think?

For some, exercising their right to speak freely can be very dangerous and require great bravery, as in Tiananmen Square, China in 1989.

Making a difference

Many people try to help others speak freely. Volunteers working with organizations like Amnesty International write letters to demand freedom for people imprisoned for their religious, political or other beliefs. Or they might **campaign** for governments around the world to release prisoners who have been imprisoned without trial.

But you can make a difference by getting information on a whole range of issues by talking with others and reading, viewing and listening to reports in a variety of different media. Only then can you establish your own opinions and begin to understand why people have different views, even if you do not agree with them. You may not always agree with your family or friends – you are entitled to an opinion and so are they.

Prejudice and inequality

We are all different. But as a species, humans have a habit of stressing the differences, and treating people badly as a result. Treating people in a negative, unequal way just because they are different from you in some respect is called **prejudice**. People are prejudiced against others for any number of reasons, including skin colour, religious beliefs, sex, age, physical abilities or **sexuality**.

Kinds of prejudice

When a person or a group of people is treated in a prejudiced way, they are not being treated as equals. Prejudice can take many forms. You might see prejudice in the playground, perhaps when someone makes a **racist** comment about another person. Disabled people may face verbal abuse but they can also face prejudice of another kind, too. When a disabled person goes to the theatre but cannot get in easily because there is no wheelchair ramp or cannot enjoy the show because there are no facilities to aid people who are hard of hearing, they are being prejudiced against because they are not being given the same chances as others.

People in power can sometimes use their positions to increase prejudice. For example, women might not be given certain jobs because the

Prejudice can come in many forms such as rallies against immigration.

employer does not consider them capable of the job or because they feel that the woman may leave to have children and be unable to commit herself to the company. Governments and leaders of some countries rule on prejudiced, often racist, lines. The **apartheid** system that operated in South Africa until 1994 separated people into different races, giving all the power and money to the white minority. Many of the world's refugees are people who have fled their homes because of prejudice that has led to persecution.

Human nature?

Many people say that their particular prejudice is justifiable. Employers who turn away female candidates complain that women they have hired in the past have been unable to do the job or were more interested in family than work commitments. People who use racial terms of abuse may say it is no different than teasing someone about their size or their hair colour. They may say that it is only natural for people to recognize differences in others. They might say, for example, that telling racist or sexist jokes is perfectly acceptable because we should all be able to laugh at ourselves, and words cannot hurt people.

A refugee camp in Iraq: the new life led by refugees has many new problems replacing those they left behind.

Others feel that even apparently small things like racist jokes can build up a culture in which a prejudice is accepted. It is only a small step to larger acts of prejudice, where certain people are not given **equal opportunities** or are even physically abused because they are different.

How do people make a difference? Many people believe prejudice and inequality is wrong. They try to treat all people fairly, regardless of their background. They complain when someone is treated unfairly. Some may support groups that demand better rights for people with disabilities, or support women's organizations, especially those working for equal opportunities. Others support organizations such as Amnesty International or Survival International, which **campaign** against the abuse of **human rights** because of ethnic background, politics or religious beliefs.

You may have suffered from or witnessed prejudice yourself. How did you deal with it?

Poverty

Poverty is a difficult word to define. It can mean different things to different people. It can mean that a person does not have enough to eat, or a proper place to live, or the other basic necessities of life. It can mean never having enough money to pay for all the other things you need – like medicines, clothes and school books. For many people, the word poverty brings to mind images of starving children living in **slums** in far-off countries. But even in countries where most people have plenty to eat and comfortable homes, there are still likely to be people who are much poorer than others. There are homeless and unemployed people in even the richest countries in the world. So poverty can mean that a person has a standard of living far below the average of the rest of the country in which they live.

What causes poverty?

Sometimes poverty may be caused by unemployment. It may be a temporary problem that will be solved when a member of the family finds work. Sometimes a person may have an illness that stops them from working full-time. In some areas there just seem to be too few jobs to go around.

In some countries there are too few **resources** to support the people living there. Many people are also affected by circumstances beyond their control, such as natural disasters, like flooding, which can destroy homes and harvests and cut them off from work and essential supplies. Sometimes the problem is that

a country is caught up in a war and is spending a large part of its income on weapons and the armed forces, instead of on provisions for its people.

Rich and poor

Some people say that many of the problems of poverty are inevitable. There is simply not enough to go around and some people are bound to suffer. Others see the differences between rich and poor as an important part of human life. After all, without competition and the desire to better ourselves, people wouldn't bother to make any effort at all. They maintain that if too much help is offered to people in need, those people won't try to help themselves. Such people argue that it is unfair to expect people who work hard for their money to give some of that money, in the form of **taxes**, to people who are too lazy to work.

POPULATION AND POVERTY

One of the reasons many people live in poverty today is the size of the world's population. As these figures show, since 1960 the world population has grown very fast. Some countries simply do not have the resources or the wealth to support the number of people living there.

1900	–	1550 million
1930	–	2070 million
1960	–	3000 million
1990	–	5300 million
2000	–	6000 million

Aid, in the form of materials and expertise, has helped these people to provide their community with clean running water.

Making a difference

The charities that work to help people in the grip of poverty have similar problems to face in the way they provide **aid**. Most charities aim to help people help themselves, rather than handing out food parcels. A charity like Oxfam, for example, works with people in poor communities to find out what they think should be done to improve the situation. Together they come up with long-term solutions such as organizing training to give people a better chance of getting a job in the future, providing people with the tools and equipment they need to set up their own businesses and offering specialist help and advice.

Others say that we live in a world where there are enough resources for everyone to live comfortably but they are not distributed evenly. They believe we have a **moral** duty to help others. They say that the rights of everyone to the bare essentials – enough food to eat, a safe place to live and access to medicines when they need them – must always outweigh the rights of others to spend their money on luxury goods they don't need. What do you think?

FACTS

- *There are more poor people in the world today than 50 years ago.*
- *The world's poorest 50 countries are home to 80 per cent of the world's people.*
- *More than 1 billion people in the world do not have clean water or sanitation.*
- *Nearly 800 million people worldwide do not get enough food.*
- *One in four people in the world cannot meet their basic needs.*

Health

The most useful single measure with which to determine quality of life is probably life expectancy – the average age to which people in each country of the world can expect to live. A woman born and living in the UK might expect to live to around 79 years old, all being well. But a woman born and living in Afghanistan or Ethiopia, would have a life expectancy of between 43 and 48 years. So what's going on?

The cost of health

Once again, the problem is money. Our health is directly affected by where we live. In the richer countries of the world, where there are more hospitals and more wide-ranging health care systems, people live longer. In poor country areas where people drink or wash in dirty water because of a lack of **sanitation**, or in smoky cities where people live in cramped housing surrounded by factories, more people become ill, more often.

Many health problems today can be treated. Scientists develop new medicines and treatments every day. Through global **vaccination** schemes we have wiped out some killer diseases of the past like smallpox. But modern medical equipment and drugs can cost vast amounts of money, and many countries can afford very little. Even in wealthier countries there is a divide between rich people who can afford expensive private treatment on demand, and those who rely on national health systems and may have to wait longer for the help they need.

AIDS, following infection by the HIV virus, is a global killer for which we have not yet found a cure. Taking drugs can lessen its effects. However, many sufferers live in the poorest countries that cannot afford the drugs. Many people say that everyone has a right to treatment regardless of their wealth, and that big drug companies should make the drugs cheaper. Others say that people with money will always have better treatment, and that is the way of the world. But should people really accept that?

Looking after your health

Many people argue that a person's health is their own responsibility. They believe that less money would have to be spent on curing diseases if people spent more time and effort looking after

This woman in Tijuana, Mexico, has no choice but to wash her clothes in a polluted river.

themselves. You can make a difference to your own health in a number of ways:

- Eat a balanced diet that includes fresh fruit and vegetables and avoid junk or processed foods.
- Drink lots of water.
- Take regular exercise e.g. walk to school.
- Make sure you're **immunized** against infectious diseases, and always check before going on holiday in case you need to be immunized before you go.
- Keep yourself, your clothes and your home clean.
- Avoid smoking, drugs and too much alcohol.

Doing these things really can make a difference, not just to you but to other people too. For instance, smokers not only risk getting diseases like lung cancer themselves, it is believed that they put others at risk too. If people were to stop smoking the cases of lung cancer would drop to a fraction of the numbers we see today, reducing misery but also easing the pressure on healthcare **resources**.

Helping other people

As individuals we can help in practical ways, by offering our time to, or by supporting charities that specialize in health issues, promote research into disorders and **campaign** for changes. Around one in five volunteers give their time to health and social welfare. There are thousands of volunteers who provide many hours of voluntary activity for hospitals each year, from visiting hospital wards to running hospital shops and cafes.

Supporting health charities is not as straightforward as it may seem. Some charities promote research into diseases that we would all like to see conquered. But what about the ways in which they do it? Some people are against research being carried out on animals for medical purposes, however good the intentions of that research might be. Others say there is simply no alternative, and that the lives of these animals are less important than the health and well-being of humans. What do you think?

FACTS

- *Every year, around 17 million people die from curable diseases.*
- *Drinking dirty water causes 80 per cent of all illness in the world.*
- *About 10 per cent of the world's population is disabled – more than 500 million people.*
- *In most countries, disabled people have less chance of getting a good education or a job.*
- *Nearly 13 million children have lost their mothers and fathers because of HIV/AIDS.*

MALNUTRITION

Malnutrition is something we often associate with poorer countries of the world. Over half of the people in the world suffer malnutrition from under-nourishment largely due to poverty. They do not get enough to eat, or they do not eat enough of the kinds of food their bodies need to stay healthy. But malnutrition simply means 'bad feeding' and it also occurs in western, developed nations. 'Over-nourishment' is where people eat too much of the wrong kinds of food. This causes them to become overweight which can lead to health problems like heart disease.

Homelessness

What do you think when you see someone huddled in blankets or sleeping bags in shop doorways? Do you assume they have run away from home or are too lazy to get a job? Millions of people throughout the world have no choice but to sleep on the streets. But those sleeping rough are only the tip of the iceberg: hundreds of thousands of people are squatting, in hostels, bed and breakfasts or other temporary accommodation. They may end up on the street for any number of reasons: abuse at home, losing their job, having no room to stay at home when grown up. Other people leave home to find their fortune in big cities; but money for accommodation and food soon runs out. Many families are without homes because a parent has lost a job and they could not make the mortgage payments and so their home may have been **repossessed**. Once you are on the street it's hard to make a change. Finding a job is difficult because many companies won't give a job to somebody who has no permanent address.

Life in temporary accommodation is often tough, especially for young people. In a one-room bed-sit it is hard for children to get enough sleep or peace to do homework, privacy is non-existent and sharing bathrooms/toilets can be difficult. Children can miss whole stretches of school because of moving between different places and so find it hard to catch up and keep friendships going.

Some homeless people find refuge in temporary shelters. Others are forced to live on the streets.

Society is changing: poverty is growing due to increasing unemployment, dependence on **credit**, breakdown of family values and poorly paid jobs where you can be better off claiming benefit rather than working. However, many people believe that the main reason there are so many homeless people is that there are simply not enough affordable, reasonable-sized homes for everyone who needs one.

VULNERABILITY

Homeless people are very vulnerable. They may end up begging for money to buy food, and risk further physical and verbal abuse from people who are angry that they are begging. They may fall into drug use and prostitution and become slaves to drug pushers and pimps. In cold or wet weather life on the streets is yet tougher, and homeless people are vulnerable to exposure and illnesses.

Making a difference

There are several charities that try to make a difference. The Big Issue Foundation helps homeless people find work, which can then help them to find somewhere to live. Others, such as Shelter and Centrepoint, aim to help people find homes. Volunteers set up emergency shelters in church halls or schools, collect blankets and give out hot food to people who can't find shelter. They also **campaign** and **lobby** governments about the dangers to people on the streets and the importance of changing laws about age limits for housing benefit. Free helplines are also vital: it can make a massive difference to be able to talk to someone who knows where to go for free temporary shelter or how to deal with abusive people on the street. Homeless people also want to get back their pride: *Big Issue* magazines are sold by homeless people who use some of the money to get themselves back on their feet.

HOMELESSNESS – A POLITICAL ISSUE?

Many people believe that charities like Shelter and the many volunteers around the country who work to help homeless people should not be necessary. Members of Parliament make decisions and laws that affect homelessness. Every year fewer new homes are built with government money. Many believe that the government should spend more money providing more and better homes for people.

Others see homeless people as at best a nuisance and at worst pathetic failures. They represent a side of society people would rather not see. In Brazil many street children are actually injured or killed each year by people wanting to clear them out of the cities. Many say homelessness will only become a thing of the past if the government plans a programme to build new homes and repair old ones to fulfil everyone's right to have somewhere safe and warm to live. What do you think?

FACTS

- *Nearly half the teenagers sleeping on the streets were once in children's homes.*
- *In the UK today there are over a million homes that are unfit to live in.*
- *200 families' homes are repossessed every day.*
- *On average eight out of ten letters to an MP are about homelessness or housing.*
- *People on the streets often die before they reach the age of 45.*
- *There are 11 million homeless people in the world.*

Children and young people

While most young people lead happy, healthy lives, many others are not getting the chances they deserve. They may not be able to go to school because their family is poor and they have to work. They may not have enough food to stay healthy because of poverty or a failed harvest. Many children's lives are damaged by bullying or abuse. Sometimes other young people may cause that abuse and sometimes parents or people in positions of authority such as teachers or doctors. Wars or natural disasters also disrupt young people's lives in many ways. They may be separated from their families, miss important years of schooling, or be physically injured.

Children's rights

There are laws that should protect children and young people under the age of 18. The United Nations Convention on the Rights of the Child was set up in 1990. This states that all children are entitled to certain rights, including the right to love and understanding, to food, housing, medical care, education, play facilities and the right to be heard. In 1991 in the UK a law was passed called the Children's Act. This aims to protect children and it gives them the right to have a say in decisions that affect them.

Children's charities

Many charities, such as the NSPCC, Save the Children and Barnardos, try to ensure that as many children as possible get the start in life they are entitled to. Other

Stepping on a landmine left over from war changed this boy's life forever.

charities, including Oxfam and the Red Cross, also help young people as well as their families.

Many charities today offer help in a crisis or emergency as well as working to find long-term solutions to problems. For instance, many children across the world – about 300,000 in total – some as young

- *There are about 2.3 billion children and young people in the world – around 40 per cent of the population.*
- *At least one child under five years old dies each week in the UK as a result of cruelty.*
- *Each week around 450,000 children are bullied at school.*
- *In developing countries, 110 million children of primary school age don't go to school and 275 million children of secondary school age don't go to secondary school.*
- *During 1998–1999 1.5 million children were killed in wars.*

as seven years old, fight in armed conflicts every day. Armies use children as soldiers in over 30 countries across the world. Some children's charities work for the immediate release of boys and girls who are being used as soldiers. At the same time they **campaign** and lobby governments to introduce tougher laws against using children in this way.

Solving problems

There are things we can all do to make a difference to young people's lives. You could start by checking your school's policy on bullying. Do they have one? If not, why not get together and help your teachers to organize a statement about bullying for everyone to read. Stand up against bullying, whether it is aimed at you or at someone else. This can be tough. You may fear you will become a target of bullying yourself. Anyone who is being bullied, or who knows someone who is being bullied, should tell an

adult – a teacher, parent or guardian. Bullying can be extremely hurtful and even dangerous. A few children have even taken their own lives because they could not stand being bullied any longer.

Look out for vulnerable children you know. They may be at risk of getting into drugs or may be affected by violence or poverty at home. Seek adult help that might make a difference to their lives.

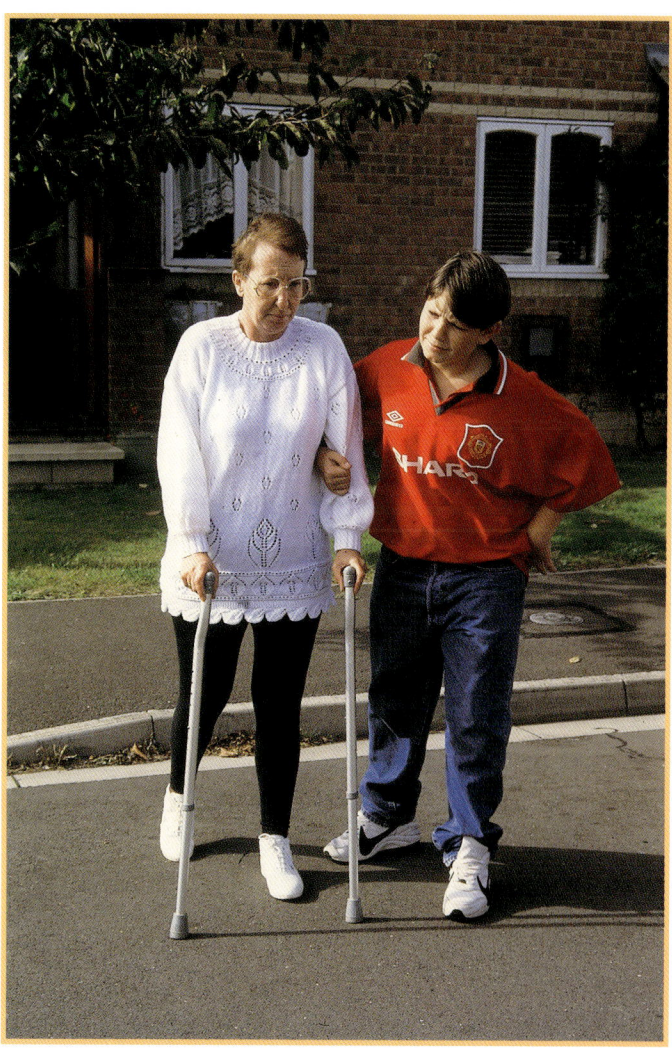

A child's schoolwork and friendships can be affected if they need to care for ill or frail members of their family.

Elderly people

In 2000 there were around 600 million people above 60 years old in the world. The percentage of older people is rising and the birth rate is dropping. Healthcare and diet are major factors in this change. **Pension** industries providing for people after they have finished work are massive operations, increasingly in the hands of the **private sector**. In the UK, for example, state pensions are quite low and increasing numbers of pensioners put pressure on the government to adjust payments. In many countries of the world, elderly people have no state pension. Many elderly people are very poor. This means that, with failing health as they get older, they are also more at risk from the cold and poor nutrition, because they are unable to afford large fuel or food bills.

Many elderly people are vulnerable to falls in the home and live in fear of attack from intruders. Half of all fatal accidents in the home happen to people over 75 years old. Older people can get very frustrated because they cannot do what they used to do.

Today, many elderly people live alone and isolated because their families are scattered throughout the country, or even the world. In Japan some older people actually pay for visits from unrelated younger families with children, because their own families live a long way away and cannot get time off work to visit them, or because they do not have grandchildren of their own. Because older people cannot always look after themselves many elderly people move into nursing homes. Living with other old people can bring great pleasure but also means learning to live in a different way. In a world where to be young can be a great bonus in terms of pop **culture**, computers and so on, advancing age can make you feel further cut off from society.

Making a difference

We can all make a difference to elderly people. We can visit the older members of our own families, helping with the shopping or bringing news of things going on in our lives. We can also volunteer our money, time and energy to help the numerous charities and voluntary groups which help old people, such as Age Concern and Help the Aged. Some volunteers run free telephone helplines, where older people can talk to experienced volunteers about money,

WHOSE RESPONSIBILITY?

Some people think a family should be able to look after its older members without relying on state handouts. Others say the state should provide unlimited help for its older **citizens** when they need it. After all, they have spent their lives working, contributing to the good of the country, fighting world wars, etc. But other people think that all governments have a budget to stick to and cannot provide for everything, and that poverty in old age is often the fault of elderly people themselves for not putting away enough savings during their working lives. What do you think?

health and safety. Other charities pay for the building of special accommodation with resident care workers and security devices like door locks, telephone alarms and smoke alarms. Simple practical help like changing light bulbs or providing a hot meal once a day makes a big difference to their lives. Activities like crafts, card games and chatting can help with the boredom that many elderly people suffer because they are too frail to lead very physically active lives. Volunteers also tell children in schools about the difficulties that old people have. In this way future generations may change their attitudes to old people. **Campaigners** push for permanent change for elderly people, perhaps asking that extra government money be available for heating in cold winters or that pensions are kept high enough.

In the developing world, the effects of poverty and disease can hit the youngest and the oldest members of societies most.

OLD DOGS CAN LEARN NEW TRICKS!

In some **cultures** elder members of society are especially valued because they have experience and knowledge of history and of past and present beliefs. Attitudes are at the heart of the problem: just because elderly people are frail, or perhaps have physical or mental difficulties does not mean they do not have something to offer others, be it experience, patience, skills, or the ability to bring history alive. Just because they are old does not mean they have no visions of their own future and that of society, and a willingness to learn new things.

Older **refugees** from wars need extra help to build their shelters and get food and water. In Africa and Asia, charities and voluntary groups provide eye care for many thousands of people with cataracts; without this help many elderly people would be unable to fend for themselves. Some charities run schemes like 'Adopt a Granny' where regular payments can provide food, shelter and medical aid as well as contributing towards new water pumps and other important things.

Elderly people can often feel lonely so a visit from a family member is always welcome.

Local issues and community care

Think of the area where you live, how it looks and the things that happen there. There might be a school and an old church nearby, perhaps a parish hall where clubs meet. Maybe there is a dangerous road that needs **traffic calming** or a neglected pond or public garden. Many crowded communities have a patch of unused wasteland somewhere. Imagine how all these things could be helped or improved.

Local voluntary groups make a big difference to community life. At schools, voluntary governors work with members of staff to make decisions about many aspects of the running of the schools, from helping to interview new teaching staff, planning and costing for the repair of school buildings, provision of music or lollipop people. Some adults offer help listening to children read or as classroom assistants. Parents and pupils volunteer their time and energy towards running school fêtes and other fundraising events like jumble sales or cake sales. As well as raising money for, say, new books or play equipment for the children at the school, such groups also play an important role in the community life of a school.

Volunteers also take part in local church and council life, considering local planning issues, making sure that village halls are not double-booked, organizing flowers and cleaning for the church. Women's Institutes pool **resources** to hold cake and plant sales, but also work to help the needier members of society.

Voluntary groups working with young people in communities, including scout, guide and beaver groups as well as youth clubs, all provide programmes and activities that develop the skills and attitudes young people need to become fulfilled and effective **citizens**. But they also provide much needed diversions from home life, which can sometimes be difficult. Youth Clubs UK trains young people to educate other young people about issues like drugs and alcohol, sexual and mental health, and healthy eating through their Peer Education scheme. It also runs YouthOrg UK, a website that helps young people and youth workers learn together.

Some voluntary schemes, like LETS, have set up a skills barter system where time and skills are given in return for other

SCOUTS AND GUIDES

The scouting movement is a worldwide organization. Robert Baden-Powell (1857–1941), an ex-army officer who had trained soldiers, first organized boys as scouts to help the British army effort during the Boer War in 1899. He then wrote his guidelines for the scouting movement for boys and later for girls. There are now 20 million scouts and guides in 150 different countries. You can learn useful skills (drama, crafts, rock climbing, canoeing, leadership… not just how to tie knots and put on a toggle!), and help vulnerable people in the community.

skills. Someone might do a couple of hours' wallpapering in return for a couple of hours' babysitting from someone else. TimeBank and Millennium Volunteers are organizations that put together people willing to volunteer some of their time and skills with charities or groups that need help in local communities. *Charlie's Garden Army* is a popular UK TV programme that shows how volunteer groups can rapidly transform public gardens in their local areas for the enjoyment of all.

But why should we give our time to local projects and activities? Do a lot of these local voluntary groups actually do much for anyone? One of the most important points is that the people who live in a place know best what might need changing. If you sit back and wait for the government or council to notice your problem, it may never be resolved. For example, you know and you care if traffic is too fast on a busy road near where you live. So you might get involved in a **campaign** for traffic calming measures. People who believe in community activity say it's also about citizenship. They argue that it is only when people work together that they get to know each other and feel part of the community and proud of its achievements. Communities can be richer places as a result of pooling knowledge and skills.

Brownies often provide entertainment for local old people's homes.

Local environment

Our local environment is important to us. It is where we spend a lot of our time and is often an extension of our home; perhaps somewhere to play, or walk, or look at animals and plants. The look of the environment and what lives in it is largely decided upon by people, either deliberately, as in a town park or garden, or as a by-product of domestic, industrial or agricultural activities. Much of the UK was once covered in forests and woodland before they were cleared to make space for animals to graze. An increasing population means that towns have gradually become cities or merged with other towns to become vast belts of buildings, cutting into the countryside around them.

Over a million tonnes of toxic waste go into landfill sites each year in the UK.

Town environments

With increasing population and industrial activity, pollution and waste is an enormous problem for towns to cope with. Liquid pollution is pumped into or accidentally spilled in rivers and seas, killing wildlife. Air pollution from exhaust fumes, aircraft and factories affect air quality, creating breathing problems, especially in young children or elderly people. **Noise pollution** from air and road traffic can make some people's lives unbearable. Some countries deal with most household rubbish collected in towns by burying it in **landfill** sites. They increasingly encourage people to separate rubbish into different materials so it can be recycled, but not everyone does this.

Countryside environments

Some people live in the countryside, but many others visit it. The challenge is to have a balance between keeping places wild or tranquil and unspoilt by people in order to support wildlife, and providing access for visitors and the people who live there. People have a right to visit and enjoy the countryside that belongs to the nation, such as National Parks and Wildlife preserves. But they also have a right to use many footpaths that cross private land, which are sometimes closed or not looked after by the landowners. Driving more and more cars into the countryside brings pollution and can kill animals as they try to cross roads. Traffic can cause problems for and frighten walkers, cyclists and horse-riders on narrow country lanes. People also demand leisure facilities in the countryside, such as campsites, nature trails, picnic areas and sports areas, which bring problems like litter and pollution.

Making a difference to environments

Some people say that surely the environment can take pollution because nature looks after itself. They might dump their rubbish in a local canal because it is out of sight. They might expect other people to clear up behind them, perhaps arguing that it is one of the reasons for paying their **taxes**. Others may ask why people should have to drive slowly on country roads just so a few cyclists can have their fun. But organizations like Friends of the Earth and The Wildlife Trusts work to lessen people's effect on environments by **campaigning** for changes, setting up new nature reserves, and highlighting and protecting **endangered species**. Friends of the Earth updates a Factory Watch website that records where industrial pollution comes from. In this way it hopes to help make people **accountable** for the mess they leave behind.

But we can all help our local environments in many ways. At the simplest level we can recycle much of our litter in bottle, paper and can banks or use it for crafts or other purposes. We can make sure we stick to footpaths in protected places. We can use our bikes to get to school safely. We can use buses and **park-and-ride** schemes in towns to help reduce car journeys. We can take part in local wildlife surveys, perhaps by counting endangered animals or plants to help estimate the size of their populations. We can help volunteer groups clear up rubbish dumped in local ponds or washed up on beaches. Every little action can help.

Animals at risk

Animal welfare issues are often in the news. Cruelty to animals is an **emotive** issue and one many people feel very strongly about. Many animals suffer because of humans. This can be as a result of accidents, for example foxes, hedgehogs and domestic pets are injured by traffic, seals are caught in fishing nets and birds are caught in oil slicks. Most people are not deliberately cruel to their pets, but some neglect them which can cause them harm. Perhaps their owners are too elderly to look after them properly, or cannot afford vets' bills or enough food. People also deliberately harm or mistreat animals. Animals are used in **laboratory** experiments, caught in traps, hunted for sport, reared in cramped factory farms or transported across the world in cramped lorries.

There are laws to protect animals from unnecessary suffering in circuses, zoos, farms and laboratories. Traps that cause unnecessary pain are illegal, and many **inhumane** sports have been banned. However, many people believe these laws do not go far enough, and some say that what laws there are, are too often ignored.

Cruelty or necessity?

Some people **campaign** to stop animals being used in ways that they see as cruel. Each year around three million animals are used in experiments, including the testing of new medical treatments and beauty products. Many companies now make beauty products without animal testing.

This bear is at risk from the people who mistreat it in order to make it perform for an audience.

But others believe that people's safety should always come before an animal's comfort and that it is foolish to be sentimental about animals. They say that keeping animals in laboratories is justified because experiments may save human lives in the future.

Fox hunting is another controversial issue. This is a traditional sport that involves foxes being chased by people on horseback and killed by a pack of dogs. Many people think that fox hunting is cruel. But fox hunters, and some farmers, say that it is necessary to control fox numbers and to stop the foxes from killing farm animals. What are your views?

Animal charities

One of the first people to make a stand against animal cruelty was Reverend Andrew Broom, a vicar from London. In 1824 he called a meeting to rally against the suffering of animals he witnessed in slaughterhouses (abattoirs). This meeting led to the formation of what became the Royal Society for the Prevention of Cruelty to Animals (RSPCA), the oldest and largest animal welfare charity in the world. There are local branches of the RSPCA all over the UK, run by volunteers.

Another famous animal charity is the World Wide Fund for Nature (WWF), founded in 1961. The organization was set up by Sir Julian Huxley, who was appalled by the **habitat** destruction and loss of species he saw on a visit to East Africa. WWF is the world's largest conservation organization. It works to protect animal species and campaigns to conserve world **resources** and habitats.

BULLFIGHTING

Bullfighting is a popular sport in Spain, parts of France and Central and South America. Matadors (bullfighters) fight a bull on foot inside a public ring. A helper stabs the bull in the neck with a spear to weaken it and so that it lowers its head. Other helpers aim coloured darts into the bull's neck. Then the matador taunts the weakened bull with a red cape to entertain the audience, before killing it with his sword. Supporters of this sport say it requires a lot of skill and the bull is killed quickly at the end. Others say that bullfighting is cruel and many campaign to have it abolished.

Helping animals

As well as volunteering to help an animal welfare charity like the RSPCA, WWF or an animal rescue centre, there are a number of very basic things you can do to help animals.

- Never drop litter. Litter can kill wild animals or damage their habitats. For example, small mammals can get trapped inside containers that have been thrown away and be unable to escape.
- Buy animal-friendly products whenever you can. This includes toiletries that are not tested on animals.
- If you see an animal in need, or you are concerned about the way someone is treating their pet, contact the RSPCA emergency line (see the end of the book for details).
- Try not to disturb animals' habitats.
- Offer to walk an elderly neighbour's dog, if they are too ill or old to give the animal proper exercise themselves.

World environment

Complex tropical ecosystems can be destroyed by loggers in a matter of hours.

towns as a result. Tropical forests and wild places, many of which provide shelter and food to increasingly rare animal species, are being destroyed at an alarming rate to clear land for human use. When the natural world is in trouble, so are we. Millions of people all over the world suffer and even die from breathing in filthy air, drinking polluted water and eating contaminated food.

Conservation organizations

There are many organizations working to conserve wildlife and the world's wild places and to protect the environment. Conservation at this level – conserving living creatures or entire **ecosystems** – is quite a challenge. The World Wide Fund for Nature (WWF) is perhaps most famous for the work it does to protect **endangered species** like the tiger and giant panda. But the charity actually does more work protecting **habitats** such as the rainforests or the world's oceans. It researches into problem areas, and then works with local people to find ways of caring for the environment while helping its people at the same time.

The **non-governmental organization (NGO)** Friends of the Earth informs people across the world about environmental problems. It also lobbies governments and industries to make changes to solve problems such as unsafe nuclear waste dumping and the building of unnecessary new roads through areas of natural beauty.

The world is under threat. Not from aliens or a speeding meteorite, but from ordinary people like you and me. The six billion people who live on this planet are slowly but surely using up its **resources** and damaging the environment to such an extent that the natural world is in serious danger. Power stations burning **fossil fuels** and cars giving off fumes cause pollution and acid rain. Forms of air pollution like this are thought to be largely responsible for climate change. Scientists predict more storms and hurricanes and changes in water levels that could endanger low-lying coastal

Greenpeace was first set up to **campaign** to stop the testing of nuclear weapons. Founder members of the organization called it 'Greenpeace' because of their vision of a 'green' (environmentally friendly) planet and peace on Earth (without the threat of nuclear war). Since then, Greenpeace has extended its activities to protect animals, plants, humans and the planet from destruction. Greenpeace is famous for its newsworthy and often daring campaigns. Greenpeace protesters scale high buildings to display protest banners and they stop the illegal testing of nuclear weapons by riding in boats in ocean test zones.

FACTS

- *Nearly one in five people in the UK is at risk from dangerous amounts of pollution.*
- *One acre of forest is destroyed every 12 seconds.*
- *Traffic fumes contain some of the most harmful substances known to humankind.*
- *Worldwide more than 1000 different species of birds and mammals are now extremely rare.*
- *Some vegetables have been found to contain 20 times the legal limits of pesticide traces.*

Making a difference

You could volunteer money or time to one of the organizations, such as Friends of the Earth, Greenpeace or WWF, that work with nature conservation. Or you could get involved in direct campaigning by writing to your local MP or the government to demand improvements in laws that protect wildlife and wild places. There are also things all of us can do in our everyday lives that would help lessen the world's environmental problems.

Many people wear masks when cycling to avoid breathing in polluting traffic fumes.

- Recycle whatever you can, including paper, tins and glass. Buy recycled paper products and other goods when you can. Try to buy less of the things you don't really need. Waste is one of the world's biggest problems.
- Don't buy exotic pets, shells, hardwood furniture or other products without first checking that their transport was legal and that they came from safe, cruelty-free or renewable sources.
- Ask your family or school if it is possible to buy at least a portion of their electricity requirements from a green energy source, such as solar or wind power. Some electricity companies will guarantee this if you are willing to pay a small amount extra. You could also encourage people to use low-energy light bulbs.

Emergencies and disasters

An emergency is a major crisis that disrupts people's lives and can even kill them. There are many different kinds of emergencies. Some are caused by natural disasters, such as floods and earthquakes. Others may be caused by people, for example wars. When there is an emergency or a disaster on a huge scale, it makes big news. You'll read about it in the newspapers and see pictures of it on your TV screens. You may also notice adverts or posters paid for by charities calling for **donations** so they can organize any help that is needed.

Emergency relief

Many charities provide aid and relief in times of crisis, including the Red Cross, Médecins sans Frontières, Oxfam, Christian Aid and Action Aid. They try to

A quick response to a flooding emergency in Mozambique saves lives.

respond quickly and appropriately to emergencies. The first job in an emergency is to save lives. Charities distribute survival packs that include things like basic cooking utensils and nappies. They also provide food, medicine, clean water and materials, such as plastic sheeting, to build shelters. Many charities today work with local people to find out what is available in the area and what people actually need. Some charities, like Oxfam, also have a store of emergency equipment that is ready to be sent anywhere in the world at a moment's notice.

EMERGENCIES AND YOUNG PEOPLE

During 1989–1999 over 12 million children lost their homes in emergencies. Children and young people are often particularly badly hit by emergencies. They may not be as strong as adults and usually rely on adults to care for them and provide food and shelter. In disaster situations families often get separated. There is also the danger that, if an emergency goes on for a long while, young people will miss out on vital months or years of education. This makes it difficult for them to lead normal lives and plan a future when the emergency does finally draw to a close.

Long-term recovery

There is usually a lot of publicity given to disasters in the first few days after they happen. With daily reminders of suffering, people are often moved to send in money or donations of clothing to help. But what happens when the world's media moves on to the next newsworthy event? The suffering has not stopped. There are still homes to rebuild and wounds to heal. This is why most charities working in crises provide two levels of support. While dealing with the immediate needs of the people involved, they are already planning what long-term recovery plans they can offer.

They may supply materials for people to rebuild their homes or community buildings, like hospitals. They may offer training in new skills or give people tools so that they have the means to earn their own living again. Some charities offer specific kinds of help. Red R is a group of volunteer engineers. They offer their special skills to communities whose buildings have been damaged, say by earthquake. They fly in and help to rebuild bridges, homes and hospitals. The main aim of many of the emergency relief charities is to help people get on with their own lives again, without having to rely on the help of others for too long.

What can you do?

There are a number of ways you can help charities that provide relief for people in times of emergency. Many of these charities, such as Oxfam and the British Red Cross, have shops where they sell second-hand donated goods, and some new items. If you are aged 13 or over you may be able to help out in a charity shop. Volunteers do such things as sorting clothes, serving customers and decorating shop windows.

You could help with fundraising activities. With the help of an adult you could take part in a street collection, where volunteers hold tins in the streets and ask people for small donations. Or you could get involved in a fundraising event, such as a book sale or a sponsored swim. Perhaps you could even organize such an event at your own school.

FACTS

- *10 million people are at constant risk from coastal floods; 3 million are made homeless*
- *40 of the 50 fastest growing cities are in earthquake zones*
- *By 2100, 60% of the world's population are predicted to live in areas affected by malaria*
- *1998 was the warmest year and had more natural disasters than any other year on record.*

Voluntary work abroad

People have different motives for volunteering to work abroad. Perhaps they want to use their skills where they are in great demand and to help others. Perhaps they want to travel, see different **cultures** or do different things, and volunteering is a way of getting a ticket. Volunteering abroad may mean you get lodging and food in exchange for the skills you offer. But it may mean that you have to pay to get there and live there as well as offering your time and skills. There are other difficulties such as the need to live and communicate with people who speak different languages and have very different cultures.

If you've got the time...

Some voluntary groups want your time and energy. Raleigh International is a youth development charity that aims to inspire people from all backgrounds and nationalities to work together on challenging environmental and community projects around the world. More than 20,000 volunteers from 72 nations have taken part in 168 Operation Raleigh expeditions to 35 different countries. Earthwatch Institute offers volunteers the chance to pay to take part in scientific expeditions around the world, such as studying mountain lion behaviour, or carrying out studies of whole **ecosystems**.

Skill seekers

Other voluntary groups want specific skills. Interested volunteers outline the skills they have to offer, the time commitments they can make, and how much notice they would need before leaving the country. VSO and Concern Worldwide are **international development** charities that apply volunteers' skills to tackling poverty in the developing world. They might, for example, send someone with teaching skills to help teach in a school in a developing country where there is a shortage of local teachers. But they will also look to change that situation by providing volunteers who can teach others how to teach, or who can advise in setting up an educational **curriculum**. This provides the developing country with the ability to provide for its own needs in the future. The emergency charity Médecins sans Frontières places 2000 qualified doctors, nurses, engineers and administrators in 70 countries each year, in order to provide medical help after war and disaster.

Increasing numbers of students take time out between study at school and study at university or college to see the world. Some find opportunities to volunteer as they travel around, perhaps helping in a mission or school they happen to visit. Others plan in advance how they will volunteer. Gap Activity Projects places volunteers in work for three to nine months of their year out, including teaching English, conservation and care work. A kibbutz is a self-supporting community based in Israel. Volunteers take working holidays carrying out agricultural labour, kitchen work and various manual duties in return for lodging and some pocket money.

Earthwatch volunteers helping study life in mangrove swamps in Belize.

Rights and wrongs

Some people say that by offering their skills abroad such volunteers are denying help to their own countries. Poverty may be obvious overseas but there is plenty of it at home. Others say that short-term voluntary help is of little use and that **resources** would be better spent on the services of a paid professional, rather than wasting money training someone for small reward. Some people say that voluntary overseas **aid**, however well meant, does not always help those in need. A developing world well project using a pump that can't be mended by local people, may end in failure because it relies on expensive, difficult-to-obtain spare parts.

A shared benefit?

People who volunteer abroad often describe their experiences as life-changing. Apart from getting to places that they'd never get to on their own and making lifelong friends with people from around the world, they can get involved in useful and **sustainable** environmental and community project work. They also share the lives of the local people with whom they work, and develop skills that will help them stand out from the crowd. Skills developed by people whilst volunteering abroad, like leadership, initiative and communication, may be very useful in gaining a job in the future, in contributing to their own community and in many other areas of life.

Volunteer views

Jenny Waldron – volunteer for the World Wide Fund for Nature

'I have been interested in wildlife since I was a child. In recent years I decided to do something positive with this interest and I joined my local WWF group. I volunteer for a wide range of activities linked to wildlife conservation. I visit schools and other local organizations to raise awareness of conservation issues and to try to encourage people to help improve the way they treat the environment.

'I take part in studies of marine life, especially dolphins and seals. This includes spending time on the cliffs nearby, taking part in Dolphin Watch, a scheme to monitor the number and health of the dolphins around our coasts.

'I also organize and take part in various fundraising activities, such as fashion shows (with second-hand clothes), sponsored walks, car boot sales and fêtes. This is a great way to extend my support for WWF as I know the funds we raise will directly benefit **endangered species** and their **habitats**, both in the rest of the UK and across the world.'

Cally Seymour-Simpson – British Red Cross Youth Member

The Red Cross is an association for both young and old people who want to help those who are sick or hurt, or who are in need in some way.

'I joined the British Red Cross when I was nine years old and I've made a lot of friends through my involvement since then. Youth members get the chance to be trained in lots of different skills. Over the time I have done various courses and earned badges as proof of the new skills I have gained. I've learnt first aid, campcraft, knots, infant and childcare, drill, fire prevention and casualty simulation. In the latter we use make-up to simulate injuries.

'I have learnt a lot about working as part of a team and I look forward to the time when I can use some of the skills I have gained in real situations.'

Toral Shah – volunteer in Oxfam shop

Oxfam opened the very first charity shop in the UK in 1947. Now there are around 830 Oxfam shops across the country. They are all run by volunteers, people of all ages who give up some of their spare time to help Oxfam.

'I started to help out because I wanted to do something worthwhile. I believe in the good work Oxfam is doing and I really wanted to make a difference.

'I usually work at the cashier desk, taking the money from people and also accepting **donations** of some of the second-hand goods that we sell. But a lot goes on behind the scenes as well. Other volunteers check the goods people bring in to see if they are good enough to sell. If they are, price tickets are attached and I put them out in the shop. Some clothes that are not good enough to sell are recycled at Wastesaver, Oxfam's big recycling centre.'

Gill Spilsbury – volunteer teacher abroad

'I first visited Nepal on a trekking holiday and the people that I met were so friendly that I knew I wanted to return. I had just retired from teaching in the UK and wanted to use my skills in a new, challenging setting. So I decided to find a school in Nepal and give something back to the country. I didn't imagine then that this would be the most satisfying teaching I have ever done.'

Bal Kunja is a small, informal residential school on the outskirts of Kathmandu. It is run by a charity called EPHC (Education, Protection and Help for Children) that offers help for children who have previously been illegally employed in carpet factories.

'The children who come to Bal Kunja have missed out on so much of what we consider a normal childhood. They have had no education, no time for play, no medical care; they even slept under the carpet looms that they worked on all day.

'Yet even with this background, the children have really positive outlooks on life and are desperate to learn. I have learnt to speak to them in Nepali so I can teach them better English. They know that once they are educated they will have a better chance of making the right choices in life.'

Pupils at Bal Kunja do not take school for granted as education can help them to have a say in their own future.

41

What can you do to make a difference?

We are all valuable members of our local and global community. We are citizens who have the right to a say in how our world is. If we don't like something, we can help to change it. It won't always happen overnight, but with enough belief, and by working with others, we can get there in the end.

Seven steps to change

1 Gather information

Inform yourself about a whole range of issues. Some you will know about already, some will be new to you. Don't just look in one book or newspaper: it is bound to have a particular opinion while possibly ignoring other points of view. Instead, go to the library and see how a whole range of media approach the issues.

Fundraising campaigns are a good way of getting involved.

2 Consolidate your thoughts

Once you have formed your views, talk with others: your family, friends and teachers. While you might not change your mind and they might not change theirs, you are likely to come to a better understanding of why people might have different views.

3 Turn thoughts into action

Find out about the ways in which you can volunteer your time, energy, skills or money as an individual or in organized groups, or both. See the addresses at the end of this book, but also check your library or school and talk with or read about other volunteers.

4 Be realistic about how much you can do

Decide how much time and energy you want to give to volunteering, taking into account your school work, leisure and sport activities and family responsibilities. Check with your parents or carers that it is OK to volunteer.

5 Get involved!

Fundraise, **campaign** by going on marches, perhaps with your family or friends, or write letters. It may seem like nothing appears to change at first. But established systems and ways of thinking and behaving can take a long time to change. Hopefully you'll have a lot of fun and enjoy making a difference.

6 Question the ways you are involved

If you feel you aren't getting there quickly enough, or if you feel a bit disheartened, maybe encourage others to join you. Or join a larger organization addressing issues of the same or similar type. Speaking with like-minded volunteers might make you question the cause, but it is likely to increase your enthusiasm.

7 Look at the wider picture

Consider the implications of what you are trying to change. Can you turn a local initiative into a national or even international one that will help many more people. Shift up a level. Instead of just fighting for temporary change at a local level, maybe campaign for permanent change on a wider scale.

Glossary

abortion ending a pregnancy by removing the foetus before it is able to survive on its own

accountable responsible for the way you behave

aid help given in the form of money or useful things (like food, medicine or shelter)

AIDS an immune deficiency syndrome that can develop after infection with the HIV virus, causing a severe loss of resistance to disease

almshouses houses for the poor provided by charity

altruistic someone who is unselfish and shows concern for others

apartheid segregation or discrimination of people based on ethnic background

campaign activity that aims to tell people something or get something changed

catalyst a person or action that first causes a change

censorship controlling the content of published material (e.g. editing out the violent bits of a film)

citizen inhabitant of a country or group of countries who has rights, such as voting and protection by the law

compassion fatigue indifference to appeals for charity due to seeing too many of them

cooperative working together towards the same goal

culture way of life, customs, and achievements of a particular group of people

currency money in general use in a country

curriculum programme of educational activities

democracy government by representatives elected by the people

demonstration gathering of people to draw attention to an issue (often carrying banners and chanting slogans)

dissent disagree

donation giving money or other useful things (e.g. to a charitable appeal)

ecosystem community of living organisms and the place and conditions in which they live

emotive arousing feeling

endangered species a type of living organism, usually in unsustainable populations, that is threatened with extinction

equal opportunities the chance to do the same things regardless of colour, sex, ethnic background, etc

ethnic with shared national or cultural traditions, sometimes applied to physical characteristics

fossil fuel oil, coal and gas, formed from the fossilized remains of once-living organisms

genetic of or relating to genes or genetics. A gene contains a particular characteristic of an organism.

global trading buying and selling worldwide

habitat place where particular living organisms live that provides for most of their needs

heritage things preserved for future generations, e.g. culture, buildings, countryside

human rights basic rights such as life, freedom of speech, education and liberty, agreed by the majority of people in the world

immunized to make immune to a disease usually by vaccination

imports goods brought into a country from a foreign country

inhumane cruel

international development aid for developing or poorer countries from developed or richer countries

kinship shared characteristics or ethnic background

laboratories scientific or medical buildings where experiments are carried out (sometimes on animals)

landfill holes in the ground where rubbish is buried

legislation laws

lobby organized attempt to influence people who create legislation, usually because of a particular shared political or moral belief

logo design used to represent a particular organization or product

militia armed force of civilians

moral concerning rights and wrongs

multigenerational spanning many different generations

noise pollution harmful or annoying levels of sound

non-governmental organization (NGO) a group whose purposes are independent of government influence

organism any living thing; an animal or plant

park-and-ride carpark with subsidized bus transport into a city centre, to avoid congestion and pollution

pension a regular payment made to people over a particular age, usually after retirement from full-time work

pharmaceutical of or relating to medicines

prejudice treating people differently, usually through ignorance of their culture or lifestyle

pressure group organization promoting a particular cause or interest, usually through lobbying

private sector part of the economy free of government control

racist person prejudiced against others because of ethnic background

refugee person escaping or sheltering from danger

repossessed taken back, e.g by bank or other creditor, because of failure to make credit payments

resources the goods and raw materials available to a country

sanitation keeping things clean, especially separating clean and dirty water

sexuality having or considering sexual relationships with others of a different (hetero-) or the same (homo-) sex

suffragette woman fighting for the right to vote

survival of the fittest survival of those best suited to their environment, often the biggest, strongest or most healthy

sustainable capable of being continued at a steady rate without exhausting the world's resources

tax financial contribution which citizens are made to pay to the government

third world debt money owed by developing countries to developed countries in return for loans

traffic calming means of slowing down vehicles (using bumps in the road or speed cameras) to make roads safer

vaccination a patient is given a mild form of a particular disease with the result that the patient is then immune to that disease

Contacts and helplines

NATIONAL CENTRE FOR VOLUNTEERING
Regents Wharf, 8 All Saints Street, London N1 9RL
020 7520 8900
Email: volunteering@thecentre.org.uk
www.volunteering.org.uk/wanttovolunteer

UK CHARITIES COMMISSION REGISTER
www.charity-commission.gov.uk

ACTION AID
Hamlyn House, Macdonald Road, Archway
London N19 5PG
020 7561 7561
Email: mail@actionaid.org.uk
www.actionaid.org.uk

AGE CONCERN (England)
Room CC00, Astral House
1268 London Road, London SW16 4EJ
020 8765 7200
www.ace.org.uk

AMNESTY INTERNATIONAL
99–119 Rosebery Avenue, London EC1R 4RE
020 7814 6200
Email: information@amnesty.org.uk
www.amnesty.org.uk

BARNARDOS
Tanner's Lane (CC), Barkingside, Ilford, Essex IG6 1QG
020 8550 8822
www.barnardo.org.uk

BIG ISSUE FOUNDATION
236–240 Pentonville Road, Kings Cross, London N1 9JY
Email: london@bigissue.com
www.bigissue.com/foundation

CENTREPOINT
Neil House (CC), 7 Whitechapel Road, London E1 1DU
020 7426 5300
Email: cathy@centrepoint.org
www.centrepoint.org

CHRISTIAN AID
35 Lower Marsh, Waterloo, London SE1 7RT
020 7620 4444
www.christian-aid.org.uk/main

COMIC RELIEF
5th Floor, 89 Albert Embankment, London SE1 7TP
020 7820 5555
Email: red@comicrelief.org.uk
www.comicrelief.org.uk/main/index

CONCERN WORLDWIDE
52–55 Lower Camden Street, Dublin 2, Eire
01 4754162
Email: info@concern.ie
www.concern.ie/ireland

EARTHWATCH INSTITUTE
Earthwatch Europe, 57 Woodstock Road, Oxford OX2 6HJ
01865 318838
www.uk.earthwatch.org/aboutew/expeditions

FRIENDS OF THE EARTH
26–28 Underwood Street, London N1 7JQ
020 7490 1555
www.foe.co.uk

GAP ACTIVITY PROJECTS
GAP Activity Projects, GAP House
44 Queens Road, Reading RG1 4BB
www.gap.org.uk/main1

GREENPEACE
Canonbury Villas, London N1 2PN
020 7865 8100
Email: supporter@uk.greenpeace.org
www.greenpeace.org.uk

HELP THE AGED
St James's Walk, Clerkenwell Green, London EC1R 0BE
020 7253 0253
www.helptheaged.org.uk

MACMILLAN CANCER RELIEF
89 Albert Embankment, London SE1 7UQ
020 7840 7840
www.macmillan.org.uk

MÉDÉCINS SANS FRONTIÈRES
124–132 Clerkenwell Road, London EC1R 5DJ
020 7713 5600
www.msf.org

MILLENNIUM VOLUNTEERS
Toucan Europe, Tanzaro House
Ardwick Green, North Manchester M12 6FZ
0161 273 5122
millenniumvolunteers.org.uk/youninfo

NSPCC
National Centre, 42 Curtain Road, London EC2A 3NH
Tel: *020 7825 2500*. Helpline: *0808 800 5000*. If you have
a hearing difficulty, call on Textphone *0800 056 0566*
www.nspcc.org.uk

OXFAM
Oxfam House, 274 Banbury Road, Oxford OX2 7DZ
01865 313600
Email: oxfam@oxfam.org.uk
www.oxfam.org.uk/get_involved

RALEIGH INTERNATIONAL
Raleigh International, 27 Parsons Green Lane
London SW6 4HZ
020 7371 8585
www.raleigh.org.uk

RED CROSS
9 Grosvenor Crescent, London SW1X 7EJ
020 7235 5454
www.redcross.org.uk

RSPCA
Causeway Street, Horsham, West Sussex RH12 1HG
01403 264181
RSPCA emergency line: *0990 555999*
Email: acockshoot@rspca.co.uk
www.rspca.co.uk

SAVE THE CHILDREN
17 Grove Lane, London SE5 8RD
020 7703 5400
www.savethechildren.org.uk

SHELTER
88 Old Street, London EC1V 9HU
020 7505 4699
Email: info@shelter.org.uk
www.shelter.org.uk

SURVIVAL INTERNATIONAL
11–15 Emerald Street, London WC1N 3QL
020 7242 1441
Email: info@survival-international.org
www.survival.org.uk

VOLUNTARY SERVICE OVERSEAS (VSO)
317 Putney Bridge Road, London SW15 2PN
020 8780 7200
www.vso.org.uk

WARCHILD
5-7 Anglers' Lane, London NW5 3DG
020 7916 9276
Email: info@warchild.globalnet.co.uk

WORLD WIDE FUND FOR NATURE (WWF-UK)
Panda House, Weyside Park, Godalming, Surrey GU7 IXR
01483 426444
wwf-uk@wwf-uk.org or www.panda.org

YOUTH CLUBS UK
2nd Floor Kirby House, 20–24 Kirby Street
London EC1N 8TS
020 7242 4045
www.youthclubs.org.uk

In Australia
AUSTRALIAN TRUST FOR CONSERVATION VOLUNTEERS
Box 423, Ballarat VIC 3353
Freecall: 1800 032 501
www.atcv.com.au

AMNESTY INTERNATIONAL AUSTRALIA
National Office
National Private Bag 23, Broadway NSW 2007
+61 2 9217 7600
www.amnesty.org

RSPCA AUSTRALIA
PO Box E369, Kingston ACT 2604
+61 2 6282 8300
www.rspca.org.au

Further reading

The Back Door Guide to Short-Term Job Adventures: Internships, Extraordinary Experiences, Seasonal Jobs, Volunteering, Work Abroad
Michael Landes
Ten Speed Press 2000

The Big Help Book: 365 Ways You Can Make a Difference by Volunteering
Alan Goodman, Fiona Smyth
Pocket Books 1994

The Total Volunteering Book
Sandra Cain and Michelle Maxwell
A & C Black 2000

Worldwide Volunteering for Young People 2000 Edition
Youth For Britain/Richard Branson 1999

Index

Titles in the *What's at issue* series include:

Hardback   0 431 03559 8

Hardback   0 431 03555 5

Hardback   0 431 03554 7

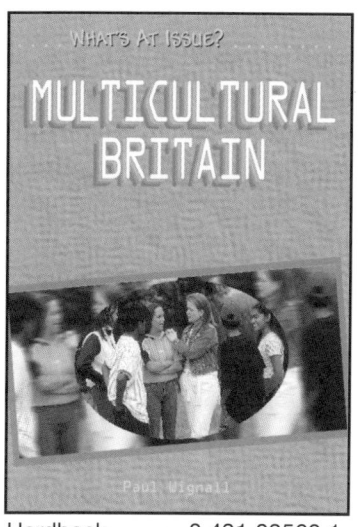

Hardback   0 431 03560 1

Hardback   0 431 03556 3

Hardback   0 431 03557 1

Hardback   0 431 03558 X

Find out about the other titles in this series on our website www.heinemann.co.uk/library